Mystical revelations receive the Imprimatur of The Church when they are judged to be in line with the Catholic doctrine and morals. An Imprimatur is Latin for "let it be printed". These revelations are meant to fill in the gaps left in the Bible because of censorship in the earlier days of the Christian Faith and also due to errors of translation. They reveal the things that happened as they happened. They are <u>not</u> meant to replace the Bible.

Books in this series

The Full of Grace: The Early Years.

The Full of Grace: The Merit.

The Full of Grace: Joseph's Passion.

The Full of Grace: The Blue Angel.

The Full of Grace: The Boyhood of Jesus.

The Chronicles of Jesus and the Apostles

Follow Me-Treasure with Seven Names

Follow Me-Where there are thorns, there also will be roses

The Chronicles of Jesus and Judas Iscariot

I see You as You are

Those who are marked

Lamb Books
Illustrated adaptations for the whole family

LAMB BOOKS

Published by Lamb Books, 2 Dalkeith Court, 45 Vincent Street, London SW1P 4HH;

UK, USA, FR, IT, SP, DE

www.lambbooks.org

First published by Lamb Books 2013
This edition
001

Text copyright @ Lamb Books Nominee, 2013

Illustrations copyright @ Lamb Books, 2013
The moral right of the author and illustrator has been asserted
All rights reserved

The author and publisher are grateful to the Centro Editoriale Valtoriano in Italy for Permission to quote from the Poem of the Man- God by Maria Valtorta, by Valtorta Publishing

Set in Bookman Old style
Printed and bound by CPI Group (UK) Ltd, Croydon, CR0, 4YY

Except in the USA, this book is sold subject to the condition that it shall not, by way of trade or otherwise, be lent, resold, hired out, or otherwise circulated without the publisher's prior consent in any form of binding or cover other than that in which it is published and without a similar condition including this condition being imposed on the subsequent purchaser

ISBN: 978-1-910201-03-9

The Full of Grace

The Blue Angel

LAMBBOOKS

Acknowledgements

The material in this book is adapted from The Mystical City of God, by Sister Mary of Jesus of Agreda, which received the Imprimatur in 1949 and also from The Poem of the Man God (The Gospel as revealed to me), first approved by Pope Pius XII in 1948, when in a meeting on February 26th 1948, witnessed by three other priests, he ordered the three priest present to "Publish this work as it is". In 1994, the Vatican heeded to the calls of Christians worldwide and have begun to examine the case for the Canonization of Maria Valtorta (Little John).

It is still the subject of much controversy, both rational and political, as are many great works. However, Faith is neither subject to rationalism nor to politics.

The Poem of the Man God was described by Pope Pius' confessor as "edifying". Mystical revelations have long been the province of priests and the religious. Now, they are accessible to all. May all who read this adaptation, which merges parts of the Mystical City of God and the Poem of the Man God, also find it edifying. Through this light, may Faith be renewed.

Special Thanks to the Centro Editoriale Valtortiano in Italy for permission to quote from the Poem of the Man God by Maria Valtorta, nick named, Little John.

Because I add no new material to these stories, I have chosen to remain anonymous.

'From Mary's Virginal Blood and Heart, the Supreme Love-Gift: Jesus-the-Eucharist.'

Mary, June 4th, 1953

Artwork by Susan Conroy.

THE CENSUS EDICT	10
THE JOURNEY TO BETHLEHEM	16
THE BIRTH OF JESUS	27
THE ADORATION OF THE SHEPHERDS	40
THE CIRCUMCISION	54
ZACHARIAH'S VISIT	61
THE PRESENTATION OF JESUS IN THE TEMPLE	68
MARY'S LULLABY	76
THE ADORATION OF THE WISE MEN	81

The Census Edict

Mary has been sitting in Her front room, working at some white linen but the greenish light coming in through the garden door is getting dark so She lays down Her work and gets up to light a lamp and shut the door.

She's now heavily pregnant; with a very big abdomen. But She's still very beautiful, as light on Her feet as a butterfly and full of dignity and grace.

Her face has matured from that of the calm innocent girl She was at the time of the Annunciation, to that of a calm and sweetly regal woman, who has reached Her full perfection in motherhood; It is now more slender, Her eyes larger and more thoughtful and it is this new slender face that She will keep forever, eternally youthful; never to know old age or the corruption of death. Thirty three years from now, when Her Son will be tortured and crucified, Her sorrow will temporarily make Her look older, like a veil thrown over Her incorruptible beauty. But when She sees Her risen Son again, the veil of age will be cast off once and for all as though when She kisses His wounds, She drinks a balm of youth which cancels the action of time. And so once again, She becomes the fresh perfect Mary She is now, like an angel; never to grow old and forever to reflect the eternal youth and eternal presence of God. A blue Angel.

Joseph, returning from an errand, comes in through the main door and Mary lifts Her head and smiles sweetly at him. Joseph smiles too but underneath, he seems worried and Mary senses this and looks at him closely.

She rises and takes Joseph's mantle from him, folds it and lays it on a chest. Joseph sits at the table, resting his elbow on it and his head on his hand. Absent-mindedly, he ruffles and combs his beard with his free hand.

'Is there something worrying you?' asks Mary 'Can I help?'

'You always comfort me, Mary. But this time, I have a big problem....that concerns You.'

'Me, Joseph. What is it?'

'They have posted an official order form Caesar Augustus on

the door of the synagogue ordering the census of all Palestinians. Everyone must go and register in his place of origin and pay his local tax. We must go to Bethlehem...'

'Oh!' exclaims Mary, laying a hand on Her enlarged bosom.

'It's a shock isn't it? And a sad one, I know!'

'No, Joseph. That's not it. I am thinking...I am thinking of the Holy Scriptures.....which say "But you Bethlehem, Ephrathah, the least of the clans of Judah, out of you will be born the Ruler". The Ruler promised to the House of David. He will be born there...'

'Do You...do you think it is already time?...oh! What shall we do?' Joseph asks in dismay, looking at Mary with pitiful eyes.

Realising how upsetting this must be for Joseph, Mary smiles reassuringly and says ' I do not know, Joseph. My time is very close but the Lord might delay it to relieve You from this worry. He can do everything. Do not fear'

'But the Journey!...Think of the crowds. Will we find lodgings? Will we come back in time? And if...if You're to become a mother there, what will we do? We do not have a home there...we do not know anyone any longer.

'Do not be afraid, everything will be all right. God finds

shelter for the animal about to give birth. Do you think He will not find one for His Messiah? We trust in Him don't we? Always....and the harder the trial, the more we trust. ...He is our guide and we rely entirely on Him...consider how He has led us with love so far....better than even the best of fathers....we are His children and His servants. We fulfil His will....this order is His will...and Caesar is only an instrument of God, Who pre-arranged events so that His Christ may be born in Bethlehem....
...Bethlehem, the smallest town in Judah did not yet exist and its glory was already destined ...-and now when the world is at peace, the glory of Bethlehem will be accomplished and the word of God come true.

.. Oh, how small are our troubles when we consider the beauty of this moment of peace! Just think, Joseph: a time when there is no hatred in the world! Can there be a better time for the rising of the "Star", the divine Light of redemption?... Do not be afraid, Joseph. If the roads are unsafe...if the crowds make the journey difficult, the angels will defend and protect us. Not us: but their king.

...if we find no accommodation, their wings will be our tents. No danger will befall us. It cannot: God is with us.'

Joseph cheers up as he listens to Her and the wrinkles on his forehead smooth out. Re-energised, he smiles and says 'You are blessed, sun of my soul! You are blessed because You see everything through the Grace of which You are full! Let us waste no more time then. We must leave as soon as possible so as to return as soon as possible because everything is ready here for the...for the...'

'For our Son Joseph. So, he must be in the eyes of the world, remember that. The Father has covered His coming with a veil of Mystery and we must not lift that veil. Jesus will do it when the time comes...' and Mary's face radiates light, beauty and sweetness when She says the name "Jesus".

And so they set about making preparations for their journey to Bethlehem, which would take five days. They prepared some vegetables, some fruit and some fish to take with them. Joseph sets out to find two donkeys to take them on the journey but it is a busy time for all of Palestine and after much enquiry, he can only find one small donkey. Mary, being fully aware of the prophecies that the Redeemer would be born in Bethlehem, also takes with Her a few linens and clothes necessary for the delivery. Having agreed on a date for their departure, they leave their home in the charge of a neighbour and set out for Bethlehem.

The Journey to Bethlehem

It's a calm winter's day. The sky is clear and the cold, sharp. On the main road, there are little donkeys everywhere, heavily loaded with people and their belongings, some going in one direction, others in the opposite direction. The people spur their mounts on, trying to hurry, also to keep warm.

Winter winds have nipped the short grass in the pastures and the bare hilly country undulating in every direction now seems more vast. The sheep in the grazing grounds stand close to ward off the cold and whilst they look for grass, they also look to the horizon at the slowly rising sun, lifting their heads and bleating as if to say to it "come quick, because it's cold"

The road runs through the centre of the valleys and slopes, going south east.
Mary is wearing a white veil, a long deep blue dress that reaches to Her feet and She's enveloped in a heavy dark blue woollen mantle, sitting sideways on a little donkey with Her little trunk in front of the saddle.

Joseph is holding the reins and walking by Her side. Unseen to human eyes, they are accompanied, guarded and defended on every side by a squadron of ten thousand angels appointed by God Himself, visible in human forms to Mary, and many others serving as ambassadors and messengers of the Eternal Father to and from His Onlybegotten, in His Mother's Womb.

Because they look poor, they are treated badly and given poor hospitality in the taverns and inns where they seek shelter during their five day journey; People are often rude to them. In some places, they are refused entry. In others, they are given a small corner in the hallway or worse. But wherever they stay, the angels form an impenetrable court around them. Because they are so well protected, Mary often urges Joseph to try and get some rest and he does. And each day, they draw nearer to Bethlehem.

'Are You tired?' Joseph asks from time to time as they approach the last stage of their journey.

'No, I am not' She answers every time. And every so often She adds ' You must be tired walking'

'Oh! Me! It's nothing for me...if I had found another donkey, You would have been more comfortable and we would have travelled faster......but take heart....we shall soon be in Bethlehem. Ephrathah is beyond that mountain.'

They travel on in silence. Mary seems to concentrate in prayer. Now and again, She smiles mildly at Her thoughts. She looks at the crowd, unseeing.

The wind rises.

'Are You cold' asks Joseph.

'No thank You.'

Joseph touches Her feet, shod in sandals and hidden beneath her long dress. He shakes his head then takes the blanket from his shoulders and spreads it on Her legs, enveloping Her arms and feet.

They travel on and meet a shepherd taking his herd from the grazing ground on the right hand side of the road to the left. Joseph stops and bending, whispers something to the shepherd who nods. Then Joseph leads the donkey into the grazing ground after the shepherd.

The Shepherd milks a big sheep with swollen udders into a course bowl and hands the bowl to Joseph who offers it to Mary. 'May God bless you both!' exclaims Mary ' you for your love and you for your kindness. I will pray for you.'

'Do you come from afar?' asks the Shepherd.

'From Nazareth' answers Joseph.
'And where are you going?' asks the shepherd again.
'To Bethlehem.'
'A long journey for a woman in Her condition. Is She your wife?'
'Yes, She is.'
'Do you have a place to go to?'
'No, we haven't'.
'That's bad! Bethlehem is crowded with people who have come from all over to register there, or are on their way to register elsewhere. I don't know whether you'll find lodgings. Are you familiar with the place?' asks the Shepherd.

'Not very.'

'Well.....I will explain it to you...for Her...' he adds, pointing to Mary. 'Find the hotel, but it will be full. But I'll tell you just the same, to guide you. It's in the largest square and this road will lead you to it. It's a long low building with a very big door. But it will be full....he says again. '...if you don't find room in the hotel or in any of the houses, go round to the back of the hotel, towards the country. There are some stables in the mountains that merchants sometimes use for their animals; they are damp and cold and there are no doors. But they are shelter because your wife...She can't be left on the road. You may find room there... And some hay to sleep on and for your donkey. May God guide you'

'And may God give you joy' says Mary.
'Peace be with you' says Joseph.

They resume their journey and climb to the top of a hill from which they can see a wider valley with surrounding slopes filled with houses. Bethlehem.

It is four O'clock on the fifth day of their journey, a Saturday, when they arrive at Bethlehem. Because it is the winter solstice, the sun is already beginning to sink.

'Here we are in David's land Mary. Now, you will be able to rest. You look so tired...'

'No. I was thinking... I think...' Mary takes Joseph's hand and says with a blissful smile ' I really think the time has come.'

'O Lord of Mercy! What shall we do?'
'Don't be afraid Joseph. Be steady. See how calm I am?'
'But you must be suffering a lot.'
'Oh! No. I am full of joy. A joy so great, so beautiful and so uncontainable that my heart is thumping and thumping and whispering to me that: "He is coming! He is coming! At every heartbeat. It's my Child knocking at my heart and saying "Mother, I am here and I am coming to give You the kiss of God". Oh! What a joy my dear Joseph!'

But Joseph is not joyful....he thinks of the urgent need to find shelter and quickens his pace. He goes from door to door asking for room but they are all full. They knock at the doors of old friends, friends of friends, all their relatives and complete strangers but everywhere they go, there is no room. In some, they receive harsh words. Others simply shut the door in their faces. And all the while, Mary, heavily pregnant and surrounded by a squadron of ten thousand angels and messengers, follow Joseph as they go from house to house and knock from door to door. In their search, they pass the public registry where they write their names and pay their taxes.

They reach the hotel but find that it is so full, even the outer porches are crowded with campers.

Joseph leaves Mary on the donkey inside the yard and goes looking for room in the other houses but comes back disheartened. The winter twilight is beginning to spread its shadows.

Joseph implores the hotel keeper
He implores some travellers.
He points out that they're all healthy men. That there's a woman about to give birth to a child.
He begs them to have mercy.
Nothing.

It is nine O'clock when Joseph returns with heart ending sorrow to Mary. All in all, they have begged at fifty different

places, been rejected and sent away from them all.
A rich Pharisee looks at them with contempt and when Mary approaches, he steps aside avoiding Her as he would a leper. Joseph looks at the Pharisee and blushes with disdain. Mary lays Her hand on his wrist 'Don't insist' She says calmly 'Let us go. God will provide.'

The angels are astonished at the wickedness of men and even more full of admiration for the patience and meekness of the tender modest Virgin exposed in Her state at Her age to the public gaze. It is from this moment on, that God begins to honour poverty and humility among men.

They go out and around the hotel wall, into a narrow street between the hotel and some poor houses and then round to the back of the hotel where they look for the stables. They find some low, damp grottos that look more like cellars but the best ones are all taken.

'Ehi! Galilean!' shouts an old man ' down there at the end, under those ruins, there's a den. It may still be free'

They hurry to the den, which is outside the city wall and find a hole in the ruins of an old building that leads into an excavation in the mountain; it's in the foundations of the old building. The roof is rubble held up with rough tree trunks and there's hardly any light.
Joseph pulls out tinder and flint and lights a lamp from his knapsack.

As he enters the hole, he is greeted by a bellow from an Ox.
'Come in Mary' says Joseph smiling. 'There is only an
Ox....It's better than nothing!'
Mary dismounts from the donkey and goes in.
Joseph hangs the lamp up on a nail in one of the supporting
trunks. There are cobwebs everywhere. The stamped
ramshackle earth is littered with rubbish, holes, excrement
and straw. From the back, an Ox, with straw hanging from its
mouth, turns it head and looks mildly with large quiet eyes.
There's a rough seat with two large stones in a corner near the
hole, blackened with sooth.

Mary is cold. She approaches the Ox and places Her hands
on its neck. The Ox seems to understand and it bellows but it
does not stir.
The Ox is eating hay from the lower tier of a two-tier manger.
And when Joseph gently pushes the Ox aside to get hay from
the upper tier to make a bed for Mary, the Ox remains calm
and quiet.
Then the Ox makes room for the little donkey that, tired and
hungry as it is, sets to eating at once. Joseph finds an
upturned battered bucket and uses it to fetch water from a
stream outside for the donkey.
Then he finds a bunch of twigs in a corner and uses them to
sweep the floor. Next, he spreads the hay out to make a bed
near the Ox, in the sheltered, dry corner. Then he finds the
hay is damp so he sighs, lights a fire and with the patience of
Job, dries the hay, one handful at a time, holding it near the

fire.

Mary, tired, is sitting on the stool. She watches and smiles.

When the hay is dry She moves over to it and sits down more comfortably on the soft Hay, with Her back against one of the supporting trunks. Joseph hangs his mantle as a curtain over the hole that is a door. Then he offers some bread and cheese to Mary and some water from a flask.

'Sleep now' he says 'I will sit up and watch the fire...there's some wood fortunately. Let us hope it will burn, and last so we can save the oil for the lamp.'

Mary lies down obediently and Joseph covers Her with Her mantle and the blanket.

'What about you...you will be cold.'

'No, Mary. I'll be near the fire. Try and rest now. Things will be better tomorrow.'

Mary shuts Her eyes.

Joseph sits on the stool near the fire with some shoots- rather few- near him.

Mary is sleeping on the right hand side with Her back to the door, half hidden by the tree trunk and the Ox, now lying on its litter.

Joseph is near the door, on the left side, facing the fire, with his back turned to Mary.

Now and again, he turns round to check on Her and sees Her lying quietly, perhaps asleep.

He breaks the shoots noiselessly, one at a time and throws them on the fire to make them last and for light and heat.

The lamp is not out and there is only the dim light from the fire which at times grows brighter or fainter. In the half light, only the whiteness of the Ox and of Joseph's hands and face can be seen.

The Birth of Jesus

Mary wakes up and looks over to where Joseph is sitting on the stool by the dying fire, his head bowed over his chest, dozing. She smiles at him, sits up and then kneels down and begins to pray with Her arms stretched out almost to the shape of a cross but slightly forward, palms up, her face in ecstasy. She remains in this position for some time then she prostrates Herself with Her face on the hay in an even more ardent prayer.

Joseph rouses and throws a handful of very slender heath on the fire reviving the flames to which he adds some twigs and sticks. It is a very cold mid-winter night and it is near to midnight, colder still because of the cold seeping in from the deserted ruins outside their cave.
Near the door where he sits, Joseph must get the worst of it and he warms first his hands over the fire then takes off his sandals and warms his feet.
Then he looks over to Mary's corner but he cannot see anything, not even Her white veil on the hay. He stands up and moves towards the pallet.

'Are you not sleeping Mary' he asks but Mary does not hear

him. He asks a second and then a third time before She turns around and replies ' I am praying.'

'Do you need anything?'
'No, Joseph.'
'Try and sleep a little. At least, try and rest.'
'I will try. But I don't get tired praying.'
'God be with You, Mary.'
'And with you, Joseph.'

Mary prostrates Herself again as before and Joseph goes on his knees by the fire and prays with his hands over his face. Now and again, he removes them to feed the fire then resumes his ardent prayer. The cave is now silent but for the crackling of the fire and the occasional stamping of the donkey's hooves. Joseph, still keeling by the fire with his hands over his face, becomes enraptured and goes into an ecstasy.

A thin ray of unearthly silver creeps in through a crack in the vault, stretching its blade as the moon rises in the sky. When it reaches Mary, it forms a halo of pure light on Her head. It is eleven O'clock of the Saturday night.

Mary hears a loud call from the Most High, raises Her head and then She goes on Her knees again. Then She raises Her head and Her face shines in the white moonlight, becoming transfigured, with a smile on Her face; She's in ecstasy. In

Her ecstasy, She is informed that the time of the Birth has arrived and all the knowledge about the Divinity and the humanity of Her Son, which She has already received from before and during the nine months of Her pregnancy, is renewed. Then She receives new knowledge of the manner in which the Birth will proceed and new light and grace on how to worthily undertake Her service to and worship of Her Son; the Almighty commands Her to treat Him as the Son of the Eternal Father and at the same time the Son of Her womb.

And the light around Her grows brighter and brighter as the angels make themselves visible in their pearl white light, preparing for the birth of the Son of God. But some of the light is coming from heaven itself, perhaps from the Throne of His Majesty Himself before Whom She kneels in ecstasy and also from the messenger angels.

But the brightest light of all seems to come from within Her. Her deep blue dress now flooded with bright white light now seems the pale blue of forget-me-nots.

Her hands and face are clear blue as though under the glare of huge pale sapphire.

And then the clear blue hue spreads itself on the things around Her, covering them, purifying and brightening everything as if paradise itself has descended into the little cave.

She is in ecstasy for an hour and the moment She issues from it, She perceives and sees that Her Son began to move and free Himself from Her womb but there are no contractions and She feels no pain, only blissful joy and delight that uplifts Her soul to heights that far surpass any ecstasy She has experienced up till now, so that She seemed entirely no longer human but entirely spiritualised.

The light from Mary's body grows stronger, absorbing the moonlight and the light descending from Heaven so that Mary becomes the Depository of all the light. It is the Light She is about to give to the world; the blissful, uncontainable, immeasurable, eternal divine Light. First, a morning star rises. Then a chorus of light points rise like a tide, and more like incense. And then they descend like a large stream and then stretch out like a veil...

The vault of the cave that was full of holes and cobwebs, of protruding rubble precariously balanced, dark, smoky and full of dung now assumes the appearance of a royal hall; each boulder is now a block of silver, each crack an opal flash, each cobweb a precious canopy interwoven with silver and diamonds. A huge green lizard hibernating between two stones now seems an emerald jewel forgotten there by a queen. A bunch of hibernating bats are now a precious onyx chandelier. The hay from the upper manger, now pure silver wires quivering in the air with the grace of loose hair.
The dark wood of the lower manger is now a block of burnished silver. The walls are covered with a brocade in which the white silk disappears under the pearly embroidery of the relief and the soil on the floor is a crystal lit up by a white light, the protrusions like roses thrown in homage, the holes, precious cups filled with perfumes and scents that rise and fill up the hall.

And the light grows brighter still. It is now so bright, it is unbearable to the eyes and Mary disappears in so much light as if She has been absorbed by an incandescent curtain.......

Within this curtain of light, the arch angels Michael and Gabriel step forth and standing at a respectful distance from where Mary is still kneeling, they assist at the Birth of Christ; the Incarnate Word penetrates the walls of the womb by divine power, leaving the virginal integrity untouched, issuing forth glorious, at the stroke of midnight turning into Sunday morning, as white incandescent light, entirely transfigured as many years later, he will be on mount Tabor. Today, his transfiguration is for Mary, so that She may see Her Son, God-Man, in His glory in order that She may understand the reverence due to Him, Whom She is to treat as a Son and also as a reward for Her love and loyalty; for Her most pure and chaste eyes that turned away from all earthly things for love of Her most holy Son. He is received with reverence into the waiting arms of the two angelic princes from where Mother and Son look upon each other for the first time and in this first look, Mary wounds with love, the heart of Her Son.

Then from the arms of the angels and still transfigured, the Infant Jesus speaks to His mother:

"Mother, become like unto Me, since on this day, for the human existence which You have today given Me, I will give You another more exalted existence in grace, absorbing Your existence as a mere creature to the likeness of Me, Who am God and Man."

And the Mother of God answers **"Trahe me post Te, curremus in odorem unguentorum tuorum."** ("Raise me elevate me, Lord, and I will run after thee in the odor of thy ointments").

And then Mary perceives the presence of the Holy Trinity in the cave and hears the Voice of the Eternal Father saying **"This is my beloved Son, in Whom I am greatly pleased and delighted"**, as he will say again at His baptism and on Mount Tabor.

Then Mary makes this request:

'Eternal Father and exalted God, Lord and Creator of the universe, give me anew Your permission and benediction to receive in my arms the desired of nations and teach me to fulfil as Your unworthy mother and lowly slave, Your holy will.'

And the Eternal Father answers:

"Receive your Onlybegotten Son, imitate Him and rear Him. And remember that you must sacrifice Him when I shall demand it from you"

'Behold the creature of Your hands; adorn me with Your grace so that Your Son and my God may receive me for his slave. And if You will come to my aid with Your Omnipotence, I shall be faithful in His service; and consider it not presumptuous of Your insignificant creature that she bears in her arms and nourishes at her breast, her own Lord and Creator.'

After this interchange, the divine Child suspends his transfiguration, suspending and confining the effects of his glory solely to His soul and now takes the appearance of one capable of suffering. In this form, Mary, still kneeling, adores Him and then receives Him into Her arms from the arms of the angels.

'My sweetest Love, Light of My eyes and Being of my soul' says Mary to Her Son 'You arrive in good hour into this world as the Sun of justice, to disperse the darkness of sin and death! True God of the true God, save Your servants and let all who seek salvation come to You. Receive me as Your slave, strengthen my shortcomings so that I may serve You as I ought. Make me, my Son, as You wish me to be in Your service.'

Then Mary offers Her Son to the Eternal Father saying 'Exalted Creator of all the universe, here is the altar and the sacrifice acceptable in Your eyes. From this hour on, O Lord, look upon the human race with mercy and in as much as we have deserved Your anger, It is now time that You be appeased in Your Son and mine. Let Your justice now come to rest and Your mercy be exalted; for on this account the Word has clothed Himself in sinful flesh and become a Brother of mortals and sinners. In this title, I recognize them as brothers and I intercede for them from my inmost soul. You, Lord, have made me the Mother of Your Onlybegotten without my merit, since this dignity is above all merit of a creature; but I partly owe to men the occasion of this incomparable good fortune since it is on their account that I am the Mother of the Word made Man and Redeemer of them all. I will not deny them my love or remit my care and watchfulness for their salvation. Receive, Eternal God, my wishes and petitions for that which is according to Your pleasure and goodwill'

Then the Mother of God blesses all men saying 'Be consoled you afflicted, rejoice you broken-hearted, rise up you fallen, rest you weary. Let the just be glad and the saints rejoice. Let the angels rejoice and the prophets and patriarchs of limbo draw new hope and let all generations praise and magnify the Lord, who renews his wonder. Come you poor,...you little ones, without fear, for in my arms I bear the Lion made lamb, the Almighty become weak, the invincible subdued. Come to draw life, hasten to obtain salvation, approach to gain eternal rest, since I have all this for all and it will be given to you freely and without envy. Do not be slow and heavy of heart, you sons of men; and You, O sweetest joy of my soul, give me permission to receive from You that kiss desired by all creatures.'

.....when the light becomes bearable once again, Mary is holding Her new born Son in Her arms. A little plum, rosy Baby. Bustling with little hands like rose buds and kicking with tiny feet that can fit in the hollow of the heart of a rose. The Baby cries with a thin trembling voice just like a new-born lamb, opening his pretty little mouth like a wild strawberry and showing a tiny tongue that trembles against the rosy roof of his mouth. And he moves his little round head in the hollow of his mummy's hand that is so blond, it looks hairless. Mary looks at Her Baby and adores Him, weeping and smiling at the same time.

Then she bends forward to kiss Him on the centre of His chest where, beneath, His little heart beats for the humanity It has come to save.....and where, one day, It will be pierced with a spear. And it seems, with Her immaculate kiss, She doctors the wound well in advance.

And because the Holy Trinity itself assisted at the Birth, heaven is emptied of its angels and they now they come forward and adore their creator in his garb of a pilgrim. And endlessly, they sing *"Gloria in excelsis Deo, et in terra pax hominibus bonae voluntatis"* in the sweetest harmonies.

The Ox, woken up by the dazzling light, now gets up with a great stamping of hooves and bellows, the donkey turns its head round and brays, recognising and adoring the Son of God, turned away and unrecognised by men.

Joseph has been enraptured and now he comes to and sees a strange light filter through his fingers held to his face. He removes his hands from his face, rises and turns round but Mary is hidden behind the Ox that stands giving warmth to the Baby but Mary calls him 'come, Joseph.'

Joseph rushes to Her but when he sees, he stops, struck by reverence and he's about to fall on his knees where he is but

Mary insists ' come Joseph' She calls again leaning on the hay with Her left hand and holding the Baby close to Her heart with Her right one.. Then She rises and goes towards Joseph who walks, halting, towards them, torn by his desire to see Him and his desire to revere Him.

They meet at the foot of the straw bed and they look at each other, weeping and smiling blissfully.

'Come, let us offer Jesus to the Father' says Mary. Joseph kneels down whilst Mary stands between two of the supporting trunks. She lifts Jesus up in Her arms and says ' here I am, on His behalf O God, I speak these words to You: here I am to do You will. And I, Mary, and My spouse, Joseph, with Him. Here are Your servants, O Lord. May we always do Your will in every hour, in every event, for Your glory and Your love.'

Then Mary bends down 'here Joseph, take Him' She says' offering him the Baby.
'What! I? ....Me? ......Oh, no! I am not worthy!' Joseph is utterly dumbfounded at the idea of touching God.
'You are worthy' Mary insists ' No one is more worthy than you are. That is why the Most High chose you. Take Him, Joseph, and hold Him while I look for the linens.'

Joseph, blushing purple, stretches out his arms and receives the Baby, Who is screaming because of the cold. When

Joseph receives the Baby in his arms, he no longer persists in his intention to hold the Baby far from himself out of respect but presses Him to his heart and bursts into tears exclaiming 'Oh! Lord! My God!' and he bends down to kiss His tiny feet.....and finds that they're cold.

He sits on the ground holding Him close to his chest then he uses his hands and his brown tunic to cover and warm the Baby, and defend Him from the biting cold and wind of the deep midwinter night. He considers moving closer to the fireplace but there's a draft of cold air coming in through the door. So he goes in between the Ox and the donkey for protection and warmth, with his back to the door, leaning over the Baby to form with his own body, a shelter, sealed on three sides; on one side, the donkey with its grey head and long ears, on the other, the Ox with its huge white muzzle, its steaming nose and its two gentle eyes.

Mary brings the linens and swaddling clothes She has fetched from Her trunk and warmed by the fire and envelops the Baby in the warm linen and then uses Her veil to protect his little head.
'Where shall we put him now' She asks.
Joseph looks around, thinking .....'Wait....' he says, '...let us move the animals and their hay over there. Then we'll take the hay up there and arrange it in here. The wood on the side will shield him from the air, the hay will serve as a pillow and the Ox will warm him a little with his breath. The Ox,

because it is more patient, and quieter than the donkey.' and he sets to rearranging the cave.

Mary lulls the baby, holding Him close to Her heart and laying Her cheek on His tiny head to warm it.

Joseph makes up the fire without economy this time and dries up the hay in the blaze, one handful at a time, holding the dried hay close to his chest to keep it warm. When he has enough for a mattress, he goes to the manger and fits it out like a cradle. 'It is ready' he says ' now he will need a blanket because the hay stings and also to cover Him.
'Take my mantle' says Mary
'You will be cold'
'Oh! It does not matter! The blanket is too coarse. The mantle is soft and warm. I am not cold at all. Don't let him suffer any longer!'
Joseph takes the soft dark blue woollen mantle, folds it in two and lays it on the hay, leaving a strip hanging out of the manger.
Now a first bed is ready for our Redeemer. Mary, with Her sweet graceful gait, comes to the manger, lays him in and covers Him with the hanging strip. She arranges it around His little head only protected from the hay by Her thin veil. Only His little face, the size of a man's fist remains uncovered.
Mary and Joseph bend over the manger, blissfully happy, and watch him sleep his first sleep, appeased now by the warmth of the clothes and of the hay.

The Adoration of the Shepherds

When the angels have all come before Him and adored the New-born Saviour, some of them are immediately dispatched to carry the happy news to different places; the arch angel Michael takes a special message from Mary to Her parents, Anne and Joachim in Limbo, where, together with the Patriarchs, Prophets, saints and the just, they await the Redemption which will open for them the gates to Paradise. For Anne and Joachim, the arch angel Michael congratulates them that their Daughter now bears the One Whom they have long awaited, and for the prophets and patriarchs, he brings them the good news of the fulfilment of what they had long ago foretold and awaited during their long banishment. There is much rejoicing and singing in acknowledgement and praise of the God-Man.

Another angel goes to Elizabeth and her son and though he is only six months old, he was pre-sanctified when the Lord, still in His Mother's womb, paid them a visit. They bow in adoration to the New-Born King and send a reply through the angel requesting that Mary adore Her Son on their behalf.

Another angel is dispatched to various corners of the earth to bring the news to those for whom it is God's pleasure to inform; to meridional Asia- present day Turkey, Afghanistan and Persia- to the Mongolian mountains and to the region where the Nile waters arise.

Back in Bethlehem, It is a calm night and the moon at its highest point, sails smoothly across a dark blue sky crowded with stars like diamond studs. Streams of light descend from the big white face of the moon onto the wide country below, making the earth white and the barren trees taller and darker against so white a background. And the low walls rising here and there along the boundaries seem white as milk, a little house in the distance seems a block of carrara marble. Inside a four sided enclosure to the right, half made of a thorn bush hedge and half of a low rugged wall, is a low wide shed, part masonry, part collapsible wood; perhaps convertible into a porch in the summer months.

From inside the shed can be heard short intermittent bleatings of little sheep dreaming or sensing the approach of dawn because of the bright moonlight. The moonlight grows stronger as though the moon were sailing closer to the earth or perhaps lit by a mysterious fire.

From the door of the shed, a shepherd looks out and up, shielding his eyes with his hands from the blinding light of the improbably bright moon that seems brighter still because he has just emerged from the dark. Surprised at the brightness of the moonlight, the shepherd calls on his companions; a group of hairy men of various ages; some grey haired, some in their teens or younger still. They crowd at the door and comment on the strangeness of the moon. Twelve year old Levi begins to cry and the older shepherds jeer at him.

'What are you afraid of, you fool?' says Elias, the oldest. 'Can't you see the air is very quiet? Have you never seen clear moonlight before? You have been tied to your mother's apron strings haven't you? But there is much for you to see...Once, I went as far as the Lebanon mountains...even further. High up. I was young and walking was good....and I was rich back then.....one night, I saw a light so bright, I thought Elijah was coming back on his chariot of fire. And an old man- he was the old man back then- said to me " a great adventure is about to take place in the world". It turned out a great misadventure because the roman soldiers came. Oh! You will see many things....if you live long enough.'

But Levi is no longer listening....and he's no longer afraid. From his hiding place behind the shoulders of a muscular herdsman, Levi leaves the threshold and goes out onto the grassy ridge in front of the shed, looking up and walking like one hypnotised. Then he shouts 'Oh!' and stops, frozen, with his arms slightly stretched out. His companions look at one another, speechless. 'What is the matter with the fool' mocks one.

'I will send him back to his mother tomorrow. I don't want mad people guarding the sheep' says another.

'Let us go and see before we judge him' says Elias. 'Wake the others and bring your sticks. It might be a wild animal or a robber...'

They fetch the other shepherds and join Levi, with torches and clubs.

'There, there...' whispers Levi, smiling. '...above the tree...look at the light that is coming. It seems to be descending on a ray of the moon. There it is, coming nearer. How beautiful it is!'

' I can only see a rather brighter light.'

'So can I.'

'So can I' say the others.

'No. I can see something like a body' says Elias.

'It is...it is an angel' shouts Levi. 'Here he is. He is coming down...he is coming near...Down! On your knees before the angel of God!'

'OOOOh!' cry the shepherds in veneration and fall face to the ground, the older ones more crushed by the shining apparition. The young ones remain kneeling, looking at the angel as he draws nearer and nearer and then stops mid-air, hovering above the wall of the enclosure; a pearly brightness in the white moonlight waving his large wings.

'Do not fear! I bring you good news. I announce a great joy for the people of Israel and of the whole world' says the angel in a voice like the harmony of a harp and the song of nightingales......'Today, in the City of David, the Saviour has been born....' says the angel, joyfully spreading out his wings wider and wider, as golden sparks and precious stones stream

from them in a triumphal rainbow arch above the shed.
'...the Saviour, Who is Christ' says the angel as he glows brighter, his wings now still and pointing upwards like two sails on flames rising up to Heaven.
'...Christ, the Lord!' finishes the angel folding his sparkling wings back onto his body, wrapping himself with them like a coat of diamonds on a dress of pearls. And he bows down in adoration, his arms crossed over his chest, his head bent down, disappearing in the shade of the tops of his folded wings and he remains motionless, a bright oblong figure for a few moments.

Then he stirs, spreads his wings again, lifts his head and with a bright heavenly smile says 'You will find him in a poor stable, behind Bethlehem; a baby in swaddling clothes, in a manger for animals ...' and the angel becomes grave '...because no roof was found for the Messiah in the City of David' he finishes sadly.

And then a ladder of angels appears, descending from heaven, rejoicing. And their heavenly brightness deems the moonlight. They gather round the announcing angel, fluttering their wings, exhaling perfumes, playing musical notes that elevate the most beautiful voices of creation to uniform perfection, to give man a hint of the beauty of God, of Paradise....

And the brightness of the angels spreads throughout the quiet country in wider and wider circles. And the birds, in the early light, join in singing. And the sheep add their bleatings for the early sun. And like the Ox and the donkey, all the animals adore and welcome their creator come among them as God and Man.

The singing and the light gradually fades away and the angels ascend to Heaven...

The Shepherds come back to themselves...
'Did you hear?'
'Shall we go and see?'
'And what about the animals?'
'Oh! Nothing will happen to them! We are going to obey God's word!...'
'But where shall we go?'
'Didn't he say that He was born today? And that they did not find lodgings in Bethlehem?' says Elias 'Come with me, I know where He is. I saw the woman and felt sorry for Her. I told them, where to go for Her sake and I gave the man some milk for Her. She is so young and beautiful ...and She must be as good and as kind as the angel who spoke to us. Come, let us go and get some milk, cheese, lambs and tanned hides. They must be very poor....and I wonder How cold He must be, Whose name I dare not mention! And Imagine! I spoke to the Mother as I might have spoken to a poor wife!...'

They go back into the shed and return shortly with little flasks of milk, small whole round cheeses in nets, bleating lambs in baskets and some tanned hides.

They close the shed and set out with torches in the moonlight on country paths among thorn bushes stripped bare by the winter. They take a back route round Bethlehem, finding the holy family first, without passing the other stables. All twelve of them approach the hole.
'Go in.'
'I wouldn't dare!'
'You go in.'
'No.'
'At least have a look.'
'You, Levi, you saw the angel first, obviously because you're better than we are. Look in'
Levi hesitates. Then he decides, approaches the hole, pulls the mantle a little to one side and looks in....and remains enraptured.
'What can you see?' they whisper anxiously.
'I can see a beautiful young woman and a man bending over a manger and I can hear...I can hear a little baby crying and the woman is speaking to him in a voice...oh! What a voice!'
'What is she saying?'
'She is saying "Jesus, little one! Jesus, love of your mummy! Don't cry, little son". She is saying: "Oh! If I could only say to You 'take some milk, little one'. But I have not got any yet". She says "You are so cold, My love! And the hay is stinging You! How painful it is for Your mummy to hear You crying

so, without being able to help You!" She says: "Sleep, soul of Mine! Because it breaks my heart to hear you crying and see Your tears!" and She kisses Him, and She must be warming His little feet with Her hands because She is bent with Her arms in the manger.'
'Call Her! Let them hear you.'
'I won't. You should call Her because you brought us here and you know Her!'
Elias opens his mouth but he only moans faintly.
Joseph turns round and comes to the door.
'Who are you?' he asks.
'Shepherds.... We brought you some food and some wool. We have come to worship the Saviour.'
'Come in.'

The older men push the young ones in front of them and they all go in, lighting the stable with their torches.
'Come' says Mary, turning round and smiling. 'Come' She says again still smiling and inviting them with Her hand. She draws Levi to Herself by the manger and he looks in and is happy. Joseph also invites the others, who come forward with their gifts and place them at Mary's feet with a few words. Then they look at the Baby Who is weeping a little and they smile, moved and happy.

'Mother, take this wool' says one of the bolder shepherds 'it is soft and clean. I prepared it for my child who is about to be born. But I offer it to You. Lay Your Son in this wool. It will be soft and warm.'

Mary accepts the thick beautiful soft white sheep wool, lifts Jesus and puts the wool around Him. Then She shows Him to the Shepherds who, kneeling, look at him ecstatically!

Now, becoming bolder, another shepherd suggests: 'He should be given a mouthful of milk. Better still, some water and honey. But we have no honey. We give it to little babies. I have seven children, and I know...'

'There is some milk here. Take it Woman.'

'But it is cold. It should be warm. Where is Elias? He has the sheep.'
But the sheep is outside with Elias who is looking in at the hole, unseen because of the darkness

'Who led you here?'
'An angel told us to come and Elias showed us the way. But where is he now?'
The sheep bleats, declaring its presence.
'Come in. You're wanted.'
Elias comes in with the sheep and they all look at him making him embarrassed.
'It's you!' says Joseph, recognising him as the shepherd who gave them milk on the way. Mary smiles at him saying 'You are good.'

They milk the sheep, deep the hem of a linen piece in the warm creamy milk and Mary moistens the lips of the Baby Who sucks the sweet cream, making them all smile. And they smile even more when Jesus falls asleep in the warm wool, with a little bit of linen still between His lips.

'But you can't stay here. It's cold and damp. And....there's too strong a smell of animals. It's not good...it's not good for the Saviour.'

'I know' agrees Mary with a deep sigh. 'But there is no room for us in Bethlehem.'
'Take heart woman. We will find You a house.'
'I will tell my mistress', says Elias ' She's good. She'll receive You even if she had to give You her own room. As soon as it is daylight, I will tell her. her house is full of people but she'll find room for You.'

'For My Child at least. Joseph and I can also lie on the floor. But for the little One....'

'Don't worry woman. We will see to it. And we will tell many people what we were told. You will lack nothing. For the time being, take what we poor shepherds can offer You....'

'We are poor too...and we cannot reward you' says Joseph.

'Oh! We don't want it! Even if you could afford it, we would not want it. The Lord has already rewarded us. He promised peace to all. The angel said: "peace to men of good will". But he has already given it to us because the angel said that this Child is the Saviour, Who is Christ, the Lord. We are poor and ignorant but we know that the Prophets say that the Saviour will be the Prince of Peace. And He told us to come and adore Him. That is why he gave us His peace. Glory be to God in the Most High Heaven and glory to His Christ here. And You are blessed, Woman, Who gave birth to Him: You are holy, because You deserved to bear Him. Give us orders as our queen because we will be glad to serve You. What can we do for You?'

'You can love My Son and always cherish the same thoughts you have now.'

'But what about You? Is there anything You wish? Have You no relatives whom You would like to inform that He has been born?'

' Yes, I have. But they are far away, in Hebron...'

'I will go' says Elias 'who are they?'

'Zachariah the priest and my cousin Elizabeth.'

'Zachariah? Oh! I know him well. I go up those mountains in

the summer months because the pastures there are rich and beautiful and I am friends with his shepherd. When I know You are settled, I will go to Zachariah.'

'Thank you Elias.'

'Please don't thank me. It is a great honour for me, a poor shepherd to go and speak to the priest and say to him: "the Saviour has been born".'

'No. You must say to him "Your cousin, Mary of Nazareth, says Jesus has been born, and that you should come to Bethlehem "'

'I will say that.'

'May God reward you. I will remember you Elias, and every one of you.'

'Will you tell your baby about us?'
'I certainly will.'

'I am Elias.'
'And I am Levi.'
'And I am Samuel.'
'And I Jonah.'
'And I Isaac.'
'And I Tobias.'

'And I Jonathan.'
'And I Daniel.'
'And I Simeon.'
'My name is John.'
'I am Joseph and my brother Benjamin. We are twins.'

'I will remember your names.'

'We must go...but we will come back...and we will bring others to worship Him.'

'How can we go back to the sheep fold leaving the Child?'
'Glory be to God, Who has shown Him to us.'

'Will You let us kiss His dress?' asks Levi with an angelic smile.
Mary lifts Jesus gently and sits with Him on the hay. Then She envelops His tiny feet in linen and offers them to be kissed. And the shepherds bow down to the ground and kiss the tiny feet veiled by the linen. Those with a beard clean it first and nearly everyone is crying. Joseph leans on the manger and adores.
When it is time to leave, the shepherds walk out backwards, leaving their hearts there...

The Circumcision

From the moment of the Annunciation, Mary has pondered upon the sufferings in store for Her sweetest Son and as Her knowledge of Scripture is profound, this sorrow, foreseen and expected, is for Her a prolonged martyrdom.

But regarding the Circumcision of Her Child, She has not yet received enlightenment on the will of the Eternal Father. Prudence and humility prevent Her from asking God or the angels who guard them at all times but She prays for enlightenment.

She knows that circumcision is a rite instituted to cleanse the new-born from original sin whereas the divine Infant is entirely free from this sin and Her maternal love longs to exempt her Son if possible but She reasons that as Her Son has come to honour and confirm his law by example and to suffer for man, he would be constrained by His burning love to undergo the pains of circumcision.

Then She consults with Joseph on the matter and they agree that the time appointed for the circumcision has arrived and as they have not received orders to the contrary, it is necessary to comply with the will of God manifested in the common law for though as God, the Incarnate Word is not subject to the law, yet as Man, and as a most perfect Teacher and Saviour, he would wish to conform with other men in the fulfilment of that law.

Joseph asks Mary how the circumcision is to take place and Mary expresses Her wish not to hand over Her Son to any other person but to hold Him Herself in Her arms. The delicacy of the Baby would make Him more sensitive to the pain than other children and so they procure some soothing medicine for His pain, a crystal vessel for the sacred relic of the circumcision and Mary prepares some linen cloths to catch the sacred blood to be shed for the first time for the redemption of man so that not one drop might be lost or fall upon the ground.

Joseph informs the priest and asks him to come to the cave where, as a fit and worthy minister, he might with his priestly hands, perform the rite.

Then Mary and Joseph take counsel concerning the name to be given the divine Infant at the Circumcision. 'My Lady' says Joseph 'When the angel informed me of this great sacrament, he also told me that Your sacred Son should be called "Jesus".'

'This same name was revealed to Me when He assumed flesh

in My womb; and thus receiving this name from the Most High through the mouth of His ministers, it is fitting that we conform in humble reverence with the infinite wisdom and that we call Him "Jesus".'

Whilst Joseph and Mary are conversing, countless angels in visible human form descend from on high, into the cave, clothed in shining garments, beautifully embroidered in red. They have palms in their hands and crowns on their heads and give out brilliance brighter than many suns. Brightest of all is the coat of arms they wear on their breasts, an engraving of the name "Jesus". The brilliance of this coat of arms outshines that of all the angels put together and the variety and the beauty of this engraving is at once rare and exquisite.

Keeping their eyes fixed on the Child in His Mother's arms, the angels split into two choirs in the cave, led by Michael and Gabriel, shining in greater splendour than the rest, carrying in their hands the name "JESUS" written on shimmering cards of incomparable beauty.

Michael and Gabriel address themselves to Mary, witnessed by Joseph, saying:

"Lady, this is the name of Your Son, written in the mind of God from all eternity for Your Onlybegotten Son, our Lord, as the sign of salvation for the human race; He shall reign triumphant upon the throne of David; His enemies will be

His footstool and His friends He shall raise to the glory of His right hand. And all this at the cost of much suffering and blood....
even now He will shed it in receiving this name....and it shall be the beginning of His suffering in Obedience to the will of His Eternal Father.....
....We all are come as ministering spirits appointed and sent by the holy Trinity to wait on the Onlybegotten of the Father and thy own.

....We are to accompany Him and minister to Him until He shall ascend triumphantly to the celestial Jerusalem and open the portals of heaven; ....afterwards we shall enjoy an especial glory beyond that of the other blessed, to whom no such commission has been given."

Joseph understands the mysteries of the Redemption more than most men but he does not understand them to the same depth as Mary.

On the day of the circumcision, the priest comes accompanied by two officials, to the cave where he finds the Infant in His Mother's arms. The priest is at first astonished by the rudeness of the dwelling but Mary welcomes them and speaks with such modesty and grace that their restraint soon turns to admiration at Her composure and noble majesty, which makes him wonder at the contrast with such poor surroundings. And he's moved to devotion and tenderness

and he proceeds with his duty to circumcise the Infant.
In the moment of His circumcision, the God- Child offers
three sacrifices of love to His
Father on behalf of mankind: He freely assumes the
condition of a sinner, subjecting Himself to a rite instituted as
a remedy for original sin. He offers His willingness to suffer
the pain of the circumcision as true and perfect man. Finally,
He offers His love for the human race, for which He sheds
this blood giving thanks to the Eternal father for giving Him a
nature capable of suffering for his glory.

The knife for the circumcision is made of flint, and the pain
caused by the wounding is severe. True to His human nature,
the Infant's sheds tears but despite the delicacy of His skin
and the coarseness of the knife, the Infants tears are mostly
caused by His sorrow caused by His supernatural knowledge
of the hard heartedness of men, more unyielding than the
flint.

These first fruits of His blood, offered by the Incarnate
Word are accepted by the Father as pledges that He would
give it all in order to extinguish the debt of the Sons of Adam.

Mary perceives these interior acts of Jesus, acting as Mother
in concert with Her Son, in His suffering. And She weeps as
in reciprocal love and compassion, Mother and Child cling to
one another.. She caresses Him at Her virginal breasts and
catches the sacred relic and the falling blood in a towel.

Then the priest asks what name they wish to give to the Child. Mary turns to Joseph and Joseph turns to Her, and then they say at the same time

"JESUS is his name."

'The parents are unanimously agreed, and great is the name which they give to the Child' says the priest.

And he enters the name unto the register of names of children. But as he is writing the name, he is suddenly moved and sheds copious tears though he cannot understand nor explain why. Then he says 'this Child will be a great Prophet of the Lord. Take great care in raising Him and tell me in what way I can relieve your needs.'

The Holy couple thank him graciously, offer him candles and some other articles and then dismiss him.
They apply the medicine they have acquired to Jesus' wounds and whilst He heals, Mary holds Him in Her arms night and day and does not part from Him for even one moment.

Zachariah's Visit

Zachariah has come to the hospitable house where the Holy Family have moved into. The land lady runs out into the lobby and meets the arriving guest. She shows him to a door, knocks and then withdraws discreetly.

Joseph opens the door and utters a cry of joy when he sees Zachariah. He takes Zachariah into a little room, as small as a corridor ' Mary is suckling the Baby. She will not be long 'says Joseph. He makes room for Zachariah on his couch ' sit down' he says 'You must be tired.'

Zachariah sits down and Joseph sits next to him.

'How is little John?' Joseph asks
'He is growing as strong as a little colt. But he is teething now and he is suffering a little which is why we did not want to bring him. It is very cold, which is why Elizabeth did not come either. She could not leave him without milk. She was very upset but the season is so harsh!'

'It is harsh indeed!' agrees Joseph.

'The man you sent me said that you were homeless when He was born. You must have suffered a lot.'

'Yes, quite a lot. But our fears were greater than our discomfort. We were afraid for the Child's health. And we had to stay there for the first days. We lacked nothing for ourselves because the shepherds spread the good news to the people of Bethlehem and many of them brought us gifts. But we had no house...not even a decent room...a bed......and Jesus cried so much, especially at night because the wind blew in from every direction. I used to light a little fire...only a little one because the smoke made Jesus cough...and it was still cold anyway. Two animals do not give much heat especially when the cold air comes in from every direction!....
....We had no warm water to wash Him with. Nor dry clothes to change Him. Yes, he suffered quite a lot!
...And Mary suffered seeing Him suffer. I suffered...so you can imagine His Mother's anguish! She fed Him with milk and tears...milk and love. Things are much better here now.
...I had made Him such a comfortable cradle and Mary had fitted it with a soft little mattress. But it's in Nazareth! Ah! If He had been born there, things would have been much different!'

'But Christ was to be born in Bethlehem. It was prophesied'

Mary hears their voices and comes in, all dressed in white wool, without a veil and holding Jesus in Her arms, asleep in

His white swaddling clothes.

Zachariah stands up reverently and bows in adoration. Then, respectfully, he approaches, bowing in homage to the Child Mary offers him. And then, still adoring Him, Zachariah takes Him, in the gesture of a priest holding up the Host already offered to men as nourishment for love and redemption....and that will be sacrificed. Then Zachariah hands Him back to Mary.

They all sit down.
Zachariah explains again to Mary, why Elizabeth has not come and how upset she was. 'In the past months, she made some linens for Your blessed Son. I brought them. They are in the wagon downstairs.' says Zachariah, rising to fetch them.

He returns with a large parcel and a small one.
Joseph relieves him of the heavier one. Zachariah takes out the gifts from the small parcel: a soft hand-woven woollen blanket, some linens and little dresses.
And from the larger parcel: some honey, some snow-white flour, butter, apples for Mary, cakes baked by Elizabeth and many other little tokens of motherly love of the grateful cousin for the young Mother.

'Please tell Elizabeth that I am very grateful to her, as I am to you too. I would have been so happy to see her, but I understand the situation. And I would also have loved to see little John...' says Mary to Zachariah.

'But you will see him in Spring. We will come and see You.'

'Nazareth is too far away' remarks Joseph.

'Nazareth? But you must stay here. The Messiah must grow up in Bethlehem. It is David's town. The Most High, through Caesar's will, brought Him to the town in David's land, the holy land of Judea. Why take him to Nazareth? You know in what opinion the Jews hold the Nazarenes. This Child is to be, in future years, the Saviour of His people. The capital town must not scorn its King because He comes from a despised land. You know as well as I do, how disapproving the Sanhedrin is and how snobbish its three main casts are......

......And then, here, near me, I will be able to help you somehow, and put all I have, not so much in the way of material things, but of moral gifts, at the service of this New Born Baby.....

....And when He is old enough to understand, I will be very happy to be His teacher...as I will be for my own son, so that later, when He grows up, He will bless me....

....We must consider that He is destined for great things.....and so He must be in a position to present Himself to the world with all the means necessary to win His game. ..

...He will certainly possess wisdom. But the simple fact that He was educated by a priest will make Him more agreeable to the difficult Pharisees and Scribes and will make His mission easier.'

Mary looks at Joseph and Joseph looks at Mary in a silent exchange of questions above the rosy innocent head of the sleeping Child. And they are questions full of sadness as Mary thinks of Her little house and Joseph, of his work. And they both wonder how they will start afresh here, where only a few days before, they were completely unknown. Here, they have none of the dear things they left at home, which they had prepared with so much love for the Child.

'How can we do that?' asks Mary 'We left everything there. Joseph has worked so hard for My Jesus, sparing neither labour nor money; he worked at night so that during the day he might work for others and thus earn enough to buy the best wood, the softest wool, the finest linen and prepare everything for Jesus......he built beehives and even worked as a mason to modify the house so that the cradle could fit in my room and remain there until Jesus had grown up and the cradle could then be replaced by a bed, because Jesus will stay with me until He is an adolescent.'

'Joseph can go and get what you left there.'

'And where will we put it? You know, Zachariah, that we are poor. We have only our work and our home. And they both enable us to live without starving. But here...perhaps we will find some work. But we will always have the problem of a house. This good woman cannot give us hospitality forever. And I cannot sacrifice Joseph more than he has already sacrificed himself for My sake!'

'Oh! Me! It's nothing for me! I am concerned with Mary's grief....Her grief in not living in Her own house...'
Two big tears well from Mary's eyes.

'I think that house must be as dear to Her as Paradise because of the mystery which was accomplished in it. I speak little but I understand a lot. I would not be upset if it wasn't for that. I will work twice as much, that's all. I am young and strong enough to work twice as much as I used to and see to everything. And if Mary does not suffer too much....and if you say that we must do so...well, here I am. I will do whatever you think is best. Provided that it will help Jesus.'

'It will certainly help. Think it over and you will see the reasons.'

'It is also said that the Messiah will be called Nazarene...' objects Mary.

'True. But at least, until He is grown up, let Him grow up in Judea. The prophet says: "And you Bethlehem Ephrathah, will be the greatest, because out of you will come the Saviour." He does not speak of Nazareth. Perhaps that title was given to Him for some reason unknown to us. But this is His land.'

'You say so, you priest, and we ...we listen to you with sad hearts and we believe you. But how painful it is! ...When shall I see that house where I became a Mother?' Asks Mary, weeping silently.

The Presentation of Jesus in the Temple

As a father is apt to repeat over and over again, that which he has enjoyed, so the law of the presentation of first-born sons was created so that the just men of Israel may forever sanctify their first born sons to God the Father, in the expectation that one of those first-born sons will be the God-Man with whom God is at once Father and One. Mary understands this and on the eve of the presentation, Mary prays to the Father saying:

'My Lord and God Most High, Father of My Lord, a festive day for heaven and earth will be that in which I shall bring and offer to You in Your holy Temple, the living Host and Treasure of Your Divinity. Rich, O my Lord and God, is this oblation and You can pour forth ,in return for it, Your mercies upon the human race; pardon sinners, console the afflicted, help the needy, enrich the poor, strengthen the weak, enlighten the blind and meet those who have strayed away. This is what I ask in offering to You, Your Onlybegotten, Who, by Your merciful condensation is also by Son. If You have given Him to Me as a God, I return Him to You as God and Man. His value is infinite and what I ask of You is much less. In opulence will I return to Your holy

Temple from which I departed poor. And My soul shall magnify You forever because Your divine right hand has shown itself towards me so liberal and powerful.'

The Holy Family sets out for the Temple accompanied as they always were by their ten thousand strong guard of angels and another four thousand sent from heaven for the occasion.

Mary, dressed in white, with a pale blue mantle and a white veil on Her head, descends carefully down an outside staircase of a modest house in Bethlehem, carrying with the greatest care in Her arms, Her Child wrapped in white cloth.

Joseph, in a light brown tunic and a mantle of the same colour, is waiting at the foot of the stairs with a small grey donkey. He looks at Mary as She approaches and smiles at Her. When Mary reaches him, he places the donkey's bridle on his left arm and takes the sleeping Child for a moment whilst Mary settles Herself on the donkey's saddle. Then he hands Jesus back to Her and they set out for the Temple in Jerusalem.

Holding the bridle in his hand, Joseph walks beside Mary, keeping the donkey on a straight clear path to keep it from stumbling. Mary spreads the edge of Her Mantle over Jesus, in Her lap, to keep Him warm. As they go, the couple speaks little but they often smile at each other. It's a winding road in a country made barren by the harsh winter and there are few travellers on the road.

They enter the town through a gate and continue over the broken pavement of the narrow road that runs slightly uphill between high houses with narrow low doors and only a few windows on the road. Overhead, many thin blue strips of sky peep through between the terraces.

There is much shouting and many people in the streets; some on foot, some on donkeys, others leading loaded donkeys and a crowd following a cumbersome camel caravan.

The Holy Family make irregular progress as the traffic causes the donkey to stop and start often and the holes in the pavement where the stones are missing cause the poor animal to jerk continuously, making uncomfortable riding for Mother and Child.

A Roman patrol passes by with a great clattering of hooves and arms and disappears beyond an arch built across a narrow stony road.
Joseph turns left into a wider, more pleasant road and the walls of Jerusalem emerge at the end of the street.
At the donkey stall near the gate, Mary dismounts,Joseph gives some coins to a little man who has approached him, for some hay and some water which he draws with a pail from, a

rustic well in the corner. He feeds the donkey and re-joins Mary and they both enter the Temple enclosure.

They go towards an arcade with merchants selling lambs and doves and money-changers. These merchants, Jesus will disperse one day. For now, Joseph buys two little white pigeons and then they make for a large, ornate side door with eight steps as all the doors seem to have, because the centre of the Temple is raised above its surroundings.

Inside, is a great hall with rectangular altars on the right and on the left. The tops of the altars are like basins with the outer rims higher than the inside by a few centimetres.
A priest approaches and Mary offers Her two little pigeons and a handful of coins and the priest sprinkles Her with some lustral water. Then She accompanies the priest into the ante chamber of the Temple.
It is a large ornate hall with sculptured angels' heads and palms adorning the columns, the walls and the ceiling. Light filters in through long narrow windows set diagonally in the walls.

Mary moves forward and stops a few meters from a flight of stairs that lead to an altar, beyond which is the Holy of Holies-the Tabernacle- where only the priests may go.
Jesus, now awake, turns His innocent eyes upon the priest Mary is offering Him to with the astonished look of infants a

few days old. The priest takes Him in his arms and climbs to the top of the stairs, at the altar.

Mary begins to pray and at once becomes immersed in an internal vision, though outwardly, She remains fully present. Joseph also feels the sweet presence of the Holy Spirit which fills him with joy and divine light.

The priest raises Jesus, arms fully stretched out, towards the Holy of Holies and Mary hears a voice in Her vision which says:

"This is My beloved Son in Whom I am well Pleased"

The presentation finished, the priest brings back the Child and hands Him to His Mother and then goes away.

A bent, little old man from amongst a group of onlookers, makes his way leaning on a stick. Simeon must be over eighty years old. He is a simple believer, a holy man, not a priest. He sees the Holy family surrounded by the light of the Holy Spirit and he comes to Mary and asks Her to give him the Child for a moment and Mary obliges him, smiling.

Simeon takes the Child, kisses Him and Jesus gives him His baby smile and looks at the old man inquisitively because the old man is crying and laughing at the same time, tears forming a sparkling embroidery running down his wrinkled face and beading in his long white beard that Jesus is reaching out to touch.

Mary and Joseph smile. And so do the others who praise the beauty of the Child.

'Behold this Child is set for the fall and for the resurrection of many in Israel. And for a sign, which shall be contradicted.' Simeon says.

And then to Mary, he adds 'And thy own soul, a sword shall pierce, that out of many hearts, thoughts may be revealed.'

When Simeon mentions the sword and the sign of contradiction, Jesus, bows his Infant head, as an interior act of obedience to the Father.

Joseph is astonished at Simeon's words whilst Mary notices Jesus's act of obedience to the Father and is deeply moved. And when Simon mentions sorrow, Her smile fades and She turns pale. Although She already knows, that word pierces Her soul and all of Mary's joy is changed into sorrow because it is in this moment that She learns more distinctly and in greater detail what sufferings and what a cruel death awaits Him; that He will be persecuted in every way, His teaching opposed not believed, His reputation though noble-of royal descent- will be despised He treated as a peasant, though He is Wisdom itself, He will be treated as Ignorant, a madman, a drunkard, a glutton, a friend of publicans and sinners, and called a false Prophet. He will be treated as a heretic, a sorcerer and called one possessed by devils for casting out devils.

He will be blindfolded, taunted, His holy face battered and desecrated. He will be called a blasphemer for claiming to be the Son of God and for which they will say He is guilty of death, He will be considered so notoriously wicked that the Jews will say to Pilate that no trial is necessary to condemn Him to death.

She moves closer to Joseph for comfort and presses Her Child to Her breast passionately.

Some in the crowd too are moved, others surprised but others, including some members of the Sanhedrin, laugh at the words of the old man, shake their heads and look at the old man with pitying glances thinking him mad.

'Woman' says Anna of Phanuel, 'He Who gave a Saviour to His people, will not lack the power to send His angel to console Your tears. The great women of Israel never lacked the help of the Lord and You are far greater than Judith and Jael. Our God will give You a heart of the most pure gold to withstand the storm of sorrow, so that You will be the greatest woman in creation: the Mother. And You Child, remember me in the hour of Your mission.'

By these two old holy people, public testimony of the coming of the Redeemer is given to the world.

Mary's Lullaby

Mary sets down Her needlework to give suck and change six month old Jesus's clothes in their little room in Bethlehem, where there's also Her loom.

Outside, the setting sun has coloured the clear sky with many golden clouds. Herds in the pastures are making their way back to their folds, browsing on the last grass of the flowery meadow, bleating with their heads lifted up.

Jesus is sleepy but a little restless as though he suffers some teething trouble or other childhood ailment.

Mary sings Him a sweet lullaby, a true Christmas Carol, in a pure clear voice to soothe Him to sleep

« Little golden clouds – seem the herds of the Lord

On the meadow full of flowers – another herd is watching.

But if I had all the herds – that exist in the world,

The lambkin dearest to Me – You would always be.

Sleep, sleep, sleep, sleep,

Cry no more...

Many glittering stars – are twinkling in the sky.

May Your sweet gentle eyes – shed no more tears.

Your eyes of sapphire – are the stars of My heart.

Your tears make Me cry – oh! cry no more.

Sleep, sleep, sleep, sleep,

Cry no more...

All the sparkling angels – that in Heaven be,

Form a wreath around You, innocent Child – enraptured by Your face.

But You're crying for Your Mummy – Mummy, Mummy, Mum.

To sing Your lullaby – lulla, lulla, lu.

Sleep, sleep, sleep, sleep,

Cry no more...

The sky will soon be red – and dawn will soon be back,
And Mummy had no rest – to ensure You do not cry.
« Mamma » when awake You'll call Me – « Son » I will reply.
A kiss of love and life – I'll give you with My breast.
Sleep, sleep, sleep, sleep,
Cry no more...

You do need Your Mummy – also if You dream of Heaven.
Come, do come! Under My veil – I will make You sleep.
My breast is Your pillow – Your cradle My arms,
Do not fear, My dear – I'm here with You... Sleep, sleep, sleep, sleep,
Cry no more...

I'll always be with You – You're the life of My heart

He is sleeping like a flower – Resting on My breast He is sleeping

Be quiet! – His Father perhaps He sees,

And the sight wipes the tears – Of my sweet Jesus.

He Sleeps, sleeps, sleeps, sleeps,

And He cries no more... »

She sings with such gracefulness and love and her voice is so indescribably pure that the sweet melody seems to invoke Paradise itself. And She rocks the cradle very gently as She sings.

But Jesus does not seem to settle so She picks Him up in Her arms, and sitting by the open window with the cradle by Her side, and swinging lightly to the rhythm of the song, She repeats the lullaby again, twice, until Jesus closes His little eyes, turns His head onto His Mother's breast and falls asleep thus, with His head resting on the cosy warmth of His Mother's breast, one hand also on Her breast near His rosy cheek and the other relaxed on Her lap. And so He sleeps, in the shade of His Mother's veil.

Then Mary gets up, carefully lays Him in the cradle, covers Him with small linens, spreads a veil to protect Him from flies and fresh air and then stays, contemplating Her sleeping treasure. She remains leaning with one hand on the cradle ready to rock it should he waken, the other resting on Her heart whilst She smiles happily as outside silence and darkness falls and creeps into Her little virginal room.

The Adoration of the Wise Men

Back to the night when Jesus was born, an angel takes the news to meridional Asia, to Mongolia and to the Nile region. Out of air, the angel makes a glorious star that though smaller than the stars of the heavens, is set closer to the earth and thus much larger to see. The star is to be a guide to bring the chosen to Bethlehem to adore. Travelling by night only, for many months, with its most beautiful light, it illuminates the night sky and by day, it mingles its light with that of the sun.

It is late night in Bethlehem, the streets are deserted and the silvery moonlight makes the small town look like a brood of chickens sleeping under the stars.

The light gets brighter, descending from an eastern sky crowded with stars so bright, so large and seemingly so low that it is possible to reach out and touch those sparkling flowers in the velvet darkness of the vault of Heaven.

A single star, far larger than the moon cruises forward across the sky of Bethlehem, eclipsing all the other stars like a queen going pass her maids in luminous glory. The star looks like a sphere of huge pale sapphire lit from within by its own sun and it sends a trail of spectral light with varying shades of opalescent opals; blond topazes, green emeralds, blood-red flashes of rubies and gentle sparkling amethysts mingle with predominant pale sapphire. The fast undulating trail that sweeps the sky is alive with all the colours of all the gemstones on the earth. But the heavenly pale sapphire hue emanating from the globe, washes over the houses, streets, grounds of Bethlehem-the Saviour's cradle- giving it a blue silvery tint that transforms the poor town into a fantastic silver town out of a fairy tale, and transforms the water in its fountains and other vessels into liquid diamond.

With a brighter radiation of light, the star comes to rest over the little house on the narrowest side of the square. But the inhabitants of the house, like the people of Bethlehem are all asleep behind closed doors. The star quickens its shining pulsations causing the trail to vibrate and undulate faster and faster in a semicircle in the night sky, drawing a net of stars full of shining colourful precious jewels in the most graceful hues and lighting up the sky in a joyful dance.

The little house is transfigured by the liquid fire of gems; the roof of the small terrace, the dark stone steps, the little door are like blocks of pure silver sprayed with diamond and pearl dust no royal palace on earth has ever, or will see the like; built for the use of angels and by the Mother of God.

But the virgin, awake, and unaware, is kneeling by Her Son's cradle praying. There are splendours in Her soul that far outdo the splendour going on outside.
From the main road, a cavalcade of harnessed horses led by hand, dromedaries and camels bearing riders or carrying loads approaches with hoof beats like rustling water that breaks against the stones of a torrent. When they reach the square, they all stop.

In this star light, the cavalcade looks a fantasy of splendour from the harnesses of the richest mounts, the clothes of the riders, their faces, their baggage.....everything shines. And the brilliance from the star increases the brilliance of the metals, leathers, silks, gems and coats. Their eyes are radiant and their mouths smiling because another splendour shines in their hearts: a splendour of supernatural joy.

Three members of the caravan dismount and walk towards the little house whilst the servants quickly steer the animals into the courtyard of the travellers' inn.
The three men prostrate themselves to the ground with their forehead, and kiss the ground. From their very rich attire, it is clear they are men of power. One of them, of a very dark complexion, who dismounted from a camel, is enveloped in sciamma -an Ethiopian garment- of bright pure silk, held at

the waist by a precious girdle that also holds a long dagger or perhaps a sword with a jewel-studded hilt.

Of the other two, who both arrived on splendid horses, one is wearing a beautiful robe with predominant yellow stripes, fashioned like a long loose cloak with a hood and cordon with very rich golden embroidery so that it looks like gold filigree.
The third man is dressed in a silk shirt that puffs out of long large trousers, narrow at the ankles and he's enveloped in a very fine shawl that looks like a flower garden, so bright are the flowers that decorate it. On his head, he wears a turban held in place by a little chain covered in diamond settings.

They finish adoring the ground outside the house where the saviour is and return to the travellers' inn where the servants have knocked and entered.

Some hours later, when the sun is bright in the afternoon sky, a servant comes out of the travellers' inn and crosses the square to the little house where he climbs the stairs and goes in. Moments later, he comes out again and goes back to the inn.

A quarter of an hour later, the three magi come out of the inn, each followed by his own servant. The magi are more richly dressed than they were the night before; their silks shine, the gems sparkle, a big bunch of feathers on a turban, is encrusted with precious chips.

As they walk solemnly across the square, a few passers-by stop and stare.

One of the servants is carrying an ornamented coffer re-enforced with engraved gold

The second servant has a beautiful chalice with a fine finish and a lid of pure gold, also finely finished.

The third servant has a low wide golden amphora with a lid shaped like a pyramid topped with a diamond.
The strain on the servants' faces shows that the gifts they bar are heavy but the servant with the coffer seems to be carrying the heaviest of them all.

They climb up the steps and enter into a room that extends from the road at the front to the back of the house. Sunlight streams in through a window at the back, through which one sees the little kitchen garden. From the doors in the other two walls, the owners of the house- a man, a woman, some boys and younger children, cast sidelong glances.

Mary is sitting with Jesus in Her lap, and Joseph standing by Her side but She rises and bows when the Magi enter.

She is wearing a long white dress reaching to Her ankles and slender wrists and Her blond plaits form a crown about Her beautiful face, now slightly more rosy from the emotion. 'May God be with you' says Mary to the Magi, Her eyes smiling sweetly.

The three Magi stop completely for a moment astonished. Then they come forward and prostrate themselves at Her feet.
Then they ask Her to sit down.

Mary asks the Magi to sit down but they remain kneeling, relaxing on their heels. The three servants bring forward the three gifts and place them in front of the Magi. Then they return to the threshold and kneel behind their masters.

The three Wise Men contemplate the nine month old Jesus, sitting on His Mother's lap, smiling and prattling in a shrill voice like a little bird. He is lively and strong and wearing a simple little white tunic from which His restless, white sandaled feet poke out. His plump little hands would like to get hold of everything. He has the most beautiful little face, with two dark blue shining eyes, dimpled cheeks and a pretty mouth that shows its first tiny teeth when He smiles. And His pretty little curls are so bright that they seem gold dust.

On behalf of all three, the oldest of the Magi explains to Mary that one night the previous December, they see an unusually bright star appear in the sky. The star is neither known nor ever mentioned in the maps of the sky before; its name is unknown because it has no name.

Born out of the bosom of God, it has flourished to tell men a blessed truth, a secret of God. But men pay no attention to it because their souls are steeped in mud. They neither lift their eyes to God, nor can they read the words that He writes with stars of fire in the vault of Heaven. May He be blessed forever.

The three Magi see the star and make great efforts to understand its meaning; happily forgoing sleep and forgetting even their food, they devote themselves entirely to studying the zodiac; the alignment of the stars, the time, the season, and the hour. And the combination of all this tells them that the name of the star is "Messiah"
And it's secret: "The Messiah has come to the world."

And they set out to worship Him, each of them unknown to the others; from the meridional Indies- that is present day Turkey, Afghanistan and Persia. The Mongolian mountain chains that are the dominion of eagles and vultures, where God speaks in the roaring winds and torrents and writes words of mystery on the immense pages of glaciers. And from where the Nile arises and flows with its green blue waters to the azure heart of the Mediterranean.

They climb mountains and valleys, cross rivers and deserts; vast oceans more dangerous than seas, travelling by night, heading towards Palestine because the star is leading them in that direction. Each of them unknown to the others. And for each of them, from three different points on earth, the star is going in that direction.
And then they meet beyond the Dead Sea where God's will has gathered them and begin to confer among themselves about what they had seen, the revelation they had received and hat their plans were, and found that their stories are identical. And so they continue together. And even though each one of them speaks in his own language, they understand one another by a miracle of the Eternal Father- an anticipation of the Pentecost miracle that will happen over thirty three years later.

They go to Jerusalem because the Messiah is to be the King of the Jews. But when they get there, the star hides itself over the sky of that city. And they feel their hearts breaking with pain. And they examine themselves to see whether they have failed to deserve God but their consciences reassure them. So they go to King Herod and ask him to tell them in what royal palace the King of the Jews was born so that they can go and adore Him.

Herod gathers the chief priests and scribes and asks them where the Messiah might be born and they answer "In Bethlehem, in Judah."

So they come towards Bethlehem and as soon as they leave the Holy City, the star reappears to them again.
The night before they enter Bethlehem, the star's brightness increases and the whole sky is ablaze.

Then the star stops over this house, swallowing up all the light of the other stars in its light. And so they understand that the Divine New-Born Baby is here.

And now, they are worshipping Him, offering their gifts and above all, their hearts, which never cease thanking God for the grace He has given them.

Neither will they ever stop loving His Son, Whose holy human body they have now seen.
Later, they plan to go back to King Herod, because he also wants to adore Him.

In the meantime, here is some gold, which befits a king.

Here is some incense, which befits a God.

He will experience the bitterness of the flesh, the bitterness of human life and the inevitable law of death. Our souls, full as they are with love, would prefer not to utter these words and would rather think that His flesh will be eternal like His Spirit is. But, Woman, if our writings, and above all, our souls are right, He is Your Son, the Saviour, the Christ of God. And so to save the world, he will have to take upon Himself, the evil of the world, of which death is one of its punishments.

This Myrrh is for that hour. So that His holy flesh may not be subject to the rot of decay but may be preserved whole until its resurrection. On account of this gift, may He remember us and save His servants by allowing them to enter His Kingdom.

In the meantime, so that we may be sanctified, will You, Mother, trust Your little one to our love so that His heavenly blessing may come down upon us whilst we kiss His feet?

Hiding the sadness caused by the words of the wise man, Mary offers the Child; she lays Him in the arms of the oldest magi who kisses Him and receives his caresses from Jesus. And then he hands Him over to the other two.

Jesus smiles and plays with their little chains and the fringes of their robes. He looks curiously at the open coffer filled with a yellow sparkling substance and smiles at the rainbow produced by the sun shining on the brilliant top of the lid of the myrrh.

Then they hand the Child back to Mary and stand up. Mary also gets up and they bow to each other after the youngest has given an order to the servant who goes out.

The three men carry on speaking for a while. They cannot make up their minds to leave the house. Tears shine in their eyes but at last they move towards the door accompanied by Mary and Joseph.

Jesus wants to get down and give His hand to the oldest of the three. And He walks thus, held by His hands by Mary and the Wise man, who both bend down to steady Him. Jesus walks with a hesitant step, like all children, and He laughs kicking His little feet on the strip of floor lit up by the sun.

The room runs the length of the house so it is some time before they reach the threshold where the magi kneel down once again and kiss Jesus' feet.

Mary, bending over the Child, takes His hand and guides it in a blessing gesture over the head of each wise man, in the sign of the cross traced by Jesus' little fingers, guided by Mary.

The magi go down the steps to their waiting caravan, where the horses studs shine in the setting sun. People have gathered in the little square to watch this unusual sight.

Joseph goes down with the magi and holds the stirrup as they each mount their horses and camel.

Mary lifts Jesus up on the wide parapet of the landing and is holding Him up against Her breast with Her arm to prevent Him from falling and Jesus laughs, clapping His hands.

Servants and masters are now all mounted and someone gives the starting command.
The magi once again bow as low as the necks of their mounts in a final gesture of homage. Joseph bows down. Mary bows and then She guides Jesus' hand again in a gesture of goodbye and blessing.

END

If you enjoyed this book, please kindly submit a review. We welcome your feedback. Thank you!

Extracts from the Sequels

The Full of Grace: The Boyhood of Jesus

....

The sounds of Joseph working in his workshop in Nazareth drift into the silence of the dining room where Mary is sewing some strips of wool She has woven Herself. The strips are about a meter and a half by three meters long, from which She plans to make a mantle for Joseph.

Ruffled hedges of little violet blue daisies in full bloom can be seen through the open door that leads into the kitchen garden, announcing autumn, although the plants in the garden are still thick and beautiful with green foliage.

Bees from two beehives leaning against a sunny wall are flying about in the bright sunshine, buzzing and dancing from the fig tree to the vines and then to the pomegranate tree laden with round fruits, some of which have already burst open from excessive growth, baring the strings of juicy rubies lined up inside the green-red caskets partitioned into yellow sections.

Jesus, His little blond head like a blaze of light, is playing under the trees with two boys His cousins James and Judas, who are about His own age. They have curly hair, but they are not blond.

One, on the contrary, has very dark curls that make his little round face seem whiter, and two most beautiful large, wide open blue violet eyes.

The other is less curly and his hair is dark brown, his eyes also brown and his complexion darker, with a pinkish hue on his cheeks.

The three children are playing shops in perfect harmony with little carts on which there are various articles: leaves, little stones, wood shavings, little pieces of wood.

Jesus is the one who buys things for His Mummy, to Whom He takes now one thing, then another one. Mary accepts all the purchases with a smile.

Then the game changes. James, one of the two cousins

proposes: ' Let us play at the Exodus from Egypt. Jesus will be Moses, I will be Aaron, and you... Mary. '

'But I am a boy! ' protests Judas.

'It does not matter. It's just the same. You are Mary, and you shall dance before the golden calf, and the golden calf is that beehive over there. '

'I'm not going to dance. I am a man and I do not want to be a woman. I am a faithful believer and I am not going to dance before an idol. '

Jesus interrupts them: 'Don't let us play that part. Let us play this other one: when Joshua is elected Moses' successor. So there will be no terrible sin of idolatry and Judas will be happy to be a man and My successor. Are you happy?'

' Yes I am, Jesus. But then You will have to die, because Moses dies afterwards. But I do not want You to die; You have always been so fond of me.'

'Everybody dies... but before dying I shall bless Israel, and since you are the only ones here, I shall bless the whole of Israel in you. '

They agree. Then there is an argument: whether the people of Israel, after so much travelling, still had the same carts which they had when leaving Egypt. There is a difference of opinion.

They apply to Mary. 'Mummy, I say that the Israelites still had the carts. James says they didn't. Judas does not know. Who is right. Do you know? '

' Yes, My Son. The nomadic people still had their carts. They repaired them when they stopped to rest. The weaker people travelled in them and also the foodstuffs and the many things which were necessary for so many people were loaded into them. With the exception of the Ark, which was carried by hand, everything else was on the carts. '

The question now answered, the children go down to the bottom of the orchard and from there, singing psalms, they come towards the house with Jesus in the lead singing psalms in His gentle silvery voice, followed by Judas and James holding a little cart elevated to the rank of Tabernacle.

But since they also have to play the part of the people, in addition to Aaron's and Joshua's, with their belts they have tied other miniature carts to their feet and thus they proceed very seriously, like real actors.

They complete the full length of the pergola and as they pass in front of the door of Mary's room, Jesus says: 'Mummy, hail the Ark when it passes by. '
Mary stands up smiling, and She bows to Her Son Who passes by, radiant in the bright sunshine.

Then Jesus clambers up the side of the mountain that forms the outer boundary of the garden, stands upright on top of the little grotto, and speaks to... Israel, repeating the orders and the promises of God. Then He appoints Joshua leader, calls him, and then Judas in his turn climbs up the cliff. Jesus-Moses encourages and blesses Judas-Joshua ....and then He asks for a... tablet (a large fig leaf), writes the canticle and reads it.
It is not quite complete, but contains a large part of it, and He seems to be reading it from the leaf. Then He dismisses Judas-Joshua who embraces Him crying. Jesus-Moses then climbs further up, right up to the edge of the cliff and from there, blesses the whole of Israel, that is the two who are prostrated on the ground. He then lies down on the short grass, closes His eyes and... dies.

When She sees Him lying still on the ground, Mary, who has been watching from the doorstep smiling, shouts: ' Jesus, Jesus! Get up! Don't lie down like that! Your

Mummy does not want to see You dead! '

Jesus gets up smiling, runs towards Her, and kisses Her. James and Judas also come down and receive Mary's caresses.

'How can Jesus remember that canticle that is so long and difficult and all those blessings? 'Asks James.

Mary smiles and answers: 'His memory is very good and He pays a lot of attention when I read. '

'I too, at school, pay attention. But then I get sleepy with all the hubbub... shall I never learn then? '

'You will learn, be good. '

There's a knock at the door and Joseph quickly walks across the orchard and the house and opens it.

'Peace to you, Alphaeus and Mary' Joseph greets his brother and sister-in-law, who have left their rustic cart and healthy looking donkey waiting in the street outside.

'And to you, and blessings!'

'Did you have a good trip?'
'Very good. And the children?'

'They are in the garden with Mary.'

But the children have come to greet their mother. And so has Mary, holding Jesus by the hand. The two sisters-in-law kiss each other.

'Have they been good?' asks Mary of Alphaeus

'Very good and very dear' answers Mary. 'Are the relatives all well?'

'Yes, they all are. They send You their regards. And they have sent You many presents from Cana; grapes, apples, cheese, eggs, honey......
And....Joseph?....I have found just what you wanted for Jesus. It is in the cart, in the round basket.' adds Mary of Alphaeus, bending over Jesus, Who is looking at her with His eyes wide open.
'.......Do you know what I have for You? .....Guess.' she asks, kissing His two strips of blue sky.

Jesus thinks, but He cannot guess......perhaps deliberately so as to give Joseph the joy of giving Him a surprise. Joseph, in fact, comes in, carrying a large round basket, lays it down on the floor in front of Jesus and unties the rope holding the lid in place and lifts it....and a little white sheep, a real flock of foam, appears, sleeping in the clean hay.

'Oh!' exclaims Jesus, joyfully surprised and happy. He's about to rush to the little animal but then turns round and runs to Joseph, who is still bending down over the basket, kisses and thanks him.

The two little cousins look with admiration at the little creature, which is now awake and lifting its little rosy head, bleating, looking for its mother. They carry it out of the basket and offer it a handful of clover and it browses, looking around with its mild eyes.

'For Me! For Me! Thank you father!' sings Jesus joyfully.

'Do you like it so much!'

'Oh! Very much!' White, clean....a little lamb....Oh!' And He throws His little arms around the sheep's neck, lays His blond head on its little head and remains thus, happy.

'I brought two more, also for you' says Alphaeus to his sons. 'But they are dark. You are not quite so tidy as Jesus and your sheep would always be untidy if they were white. They will be your herd; you will keep them together and so you will no longer loiter in the streets, you two little rascals, throwing stones at each other.'

Judas and James both run to the cart and look at the other two little sheep, which are more black than white, whilst Jesus takes his sheep into the garden, gives it some water to drink and the little pet follows Him as if it had known Him forever. Jesus beckons to it and calls it "Snow" and the sheep bleats happily in answer.

The guests sit at the table and Mary offers them some bread, some olives, some cheese and a jug of liquid of a very pale colour which might be cider or some water sweetened with honey.

The adults converse whilst the three boys play with their pets that Jesus wants gathered together so He can give them water and a name.
'Yours, Judas, will be called "Star" because it has that mark on its forehead.......And the name of yours will be "Flame" because it has the blazing colours of certain withering heathers.'

'Agreed.'

The adults are talking and Alphaeus says 'I hope I have solved the matter of the boys' quarrels. I got the idea from your request, Joseph. I said to myself: "My brother wants a little sheep for Jesus so He may have something to play with. I will get two more for those naughty boys to keep them quiet a little and avoid continuous arguments with other parents over bruised heads and skinned knees....with the school and with the sheep, I will manage to keep them quiet." But this year, You also, will have to send Jesus to school. It is time'

'I will never send Jesus to school.' says Mary resolutely. It is quite unusual to hear Her talk thus and even more so, to hear Her talk before Joseph.

'Why? The Child must learn to be ready in good time to pass His exam when He comes of age...'

'The Child will be ready. But He will not go to school. That is quite definite.'

'You will be the only woman in Israel to do that.'

'I will be the only one. But that is what I am going to do. Isn't that right Joseph.'

'Yes, that's correct. There is no need for Jesus to go to school. Mary was brought up in the Temple and She knows the law as well as any Doctor. She will be His Teacher. That's what I want too.'

'You are spoiling the Boy.'

'You cannot say that. He is the best boy in Nazareth. Have you ever heard Him cry, or be naughty, or be disobedient or lack respect?'

'No. That's true. But He will do all that if You continue to spoil Him.'

'You do not necessarily spoil Your children just because you keep them at home. To keep them at home implies loving them with good common sense and wholeheartedly. And that is how we love our Jesus. And since Mary is better educated than a teacher, She will be Jesus' Teacher.'

' And when your Jesus is a Man, He will be like a silly little woman frightened even of flies.'

'He will not. Mary is a strong Woman and She will give Him a manly education. I am not a coward and I can give Him man-like examples. Jesus is a creature without any physical or moral faults. He will, therefore, grow up, upright and strong, both in His body and in His spirit. You can be sure of that, Alphaeus. ....He will not be a disgrace to the family......In any case, that is what I have decided and that is all.'

'Perhaps Mary has decided and you...'

'And if it were so? Is it not fair that two who love each other, should have the same thoughts and the same wishes, so that each may accept the wishes of the other as if they were his own?... If Mary should wish silly things, I would say to Her "No." But She is asking for something that is full of wisdom and I agree, and I make it my own. We love each other, we do as we did the first day, and we shall go on doing so as long as we live. Is that right Mary?'

'Yes, Joseph. And let us hope it will never happen, but when one should die without the other, we will still go on loving each other.'

Joseph gives Mary a pat on the head as though She were a young daughter and She looks at him with Her serene loving eyes.

'You are quite right' Agrees Mary of Alphaeus. 'I wish I could teach! Our children learn both good and evil at school. At home, they only learn what is good. But I do not know whether.....if Mary...'

'What is it you want, My sister-in-law? Speak freely. You know that I love you and I am happy when I can do something that pleases you.'

'I was thinking....James and Judas are only a little older than Jesus. They are already going to school....for what they have learned!....Jesus instead, already knows the law so well....I would like....eh, I mean, if I asked You to take them as well, when You teach Jesus? I think they would behave better and be better educated. After all, they are cousins, and it is only fair that they should love one another like brothers. Oh! I would be so happy!'

'If Joseph wants, and your husband agrees, I am quite willing. It is the same to speak to one as to speak to three. And it is a joy to go through the whole Bible. Let them come.'

The three children, who have come in quietly, are listening and awaiting the final decision.

'They will drive You to despair, Mary.' says Alphaeus.

'No! They are always good with Me. You will be good if I teach you, will you not?'

The two boys approach and stand on either side of Mary, place their arms around Her shoulders, lean their little heads on Her shoulders and promise all the good in the world.

'Let them try, Alphaeus, and let Me try. I am sure you will not be dissatisfied with the test. They can come every day from the sixth hour (noon) until evening(6pm-Sundown). It will be enough, believe Me. I know how to teach without tiring them. You must hold their attention and let them relax at the same time. You must understand them, love them and be loved by them, if you wish to get good results. ....And you will love Me, will you not?

And Mary receives two big kisses in answer.

'See?'

' I see. I can only say: "Thank You." And what will Jesus say when He sees His Mummy busy with others? What do You say, Jesus?'

' I say: "Happy are those who listen to Her and build their dwelling near Hers." As for Wisdom, happy are those who are My Mother's friends, and I am happy that those who, I love are Her friends.'

'But who puts such words on the lips of the Child?' asks Alphaeus, astonished.

'Nobody, brother. Nobody in this world.'

And so Mary becomes the Teacher of Jesus, Judas and James and the three boys, cousins, grow to love one another like brothers, growing up together, "like three shoots supported by one pole"......Jesus is Her pupil exactly like His cousins are. And through this semblance of a normal life, the "seal" is kept on God's secret against the investigations of the Evil One.

www.ingramcontent.com/pod-product-compliance
Lightning Source LLC
Chambersburg PA
CBHW061333040426
42444CB00011B/2902